ABOUT THE AUTHOR

M. L. WALSH is a performance poet specializing in comedic absurdism and the construction of narrative through voice and characterisation. Her poetic monologues experiment with the translation of poetry from stage to page and how theatrical technique (and its removal) can modify a text.

Since graduating from the University of Birmingham with an MA in Creative Writing, she has headlined numerous venues inside and outside of the city including the Birmingham Glee Club.

Alongside her work in performance poetry, M. L. WALSH has established herself as an events organiser and host, with her co-organised pop-up event: The Big Gay Poetry Night debuting at the Heath Bookshop Literature and Music Festival in April 2024.

My Dog Has Never Read This is her debut full collection.

MY DOG HAS NEVER! READ THIS

M . L . WALSH

VERVE
POETRY PRESS

BIRMINGHAM

PUBLISHED BY VERVE POETRY PRESS
https://vervepoetrypress.com
mail@vervepoetrypress.com

FIRST PUBLISHED MAR 2025

Printed and bound in the UK
by ImprintDigital, Exeter

ISBN: 978-1-913917-65-4

Cover photography: Connor Pope

UNDEDICATED

CONTENTS

DISCLAIMER:

I must begin with a disclaimer. I must clarify that,
regardless of how things might appear, I do not have a
fish fetish. I don't even like fish. I hate them. I won't go
near them, not even for a snack. The line between
vegetarian (no food with a face) and pescetarian (no
food with a face unless the food with a face has fins)
is perilous to cross. Peskys know this. It is something
they are ashamed of. Some will try and tell you that
they are vegetarian. Those people are frail. And
probably have a fish fetish themselves. They are
dishonest. I am not. So, you can trust me when I tell
you that I do not have a fish fetish. The proof? Let me
ask: have you ever wrapped your lips around society's
feeble attempt at recreating the fish finger? *Without*
the fish? The *fishless* fishfinger? Yes. No? Try one.
And when you have, come back here. And we will both
agree that the person who has resigned
themselves to consuming that congealed muck for the
rest of their sad, sad existence most definitely does not
have a fish fetish. And you'd be right. I don't. Having a
fish fetish would be disturbed and perverted and
impractical. Fine. I am partial to light choking. But

not drawn, in particular, to suffocation – a fate guaranteed for at least half of those engaged in fish fetish canoodling. Something I myself have never experienced. To do so I would have to have a fish fetish. Which I don't. So, you can stop looking at me like that. Like I have one. I don't.

But have you ever seen Shark Tail (2004)?

MY DOG
HAS NEVER!
READ THIS

PART ONE: CREATION OF THE POLY-POO

Last week on his evening walk my dog ate a load of polystyrene. And when I went to pick up his shit using a small green plastic bag the shit floated away before I could get a grip on it. And my dog points at the shit, as it floats among the planes and the pigeons and the hot air balloons. He says: 'I made that.'

Took him a week to break the bad news. Caught him in bed watching Love Island (2019). Told him not to worry. Said we'd all gone through it. And that some of us would go back to it. And that some people would never stop watching Love Island (2019) because they would never get the help that they deserved. Told him not to worry. That he had the help he deserved in us.

Told him none of it. He is a dog.

SORRY!

DON'T MEAN
TO ALARM
U!

BUT YOUR LIVING ROOM IS SET OUT LIKE A THERAPIST'S OFFICE.

CAN'T SEE, WANT TO SEE, DON'T LIKE LOOKING!

In the past week I have found myself to be very frustrating. In seven days, I have gone through seven - make that three - pairs of sunglasses.

I was going to say seven. But I forgot my tendency to forget my lies.

When I was six, I heard a quote that stuck with me:

'A lie is like a ghost. It will always come back to haunt you.'

Wish my sunglasses would do the same.

The first pair perished in a flamboyant hand movement. In the moments leading up to their demise I had been chewing on one of the frames and once my friend said something particularly stupid, I flung my hand out like-

And looked down to find my sunglasses had split down the middle.

The situation was at first not critical. The same friend described to me a way to fix the glasses with superglue. But at that point I had grown distracted thinking it might be fun to walk round with a monocle.

The other two deaths were much less ceremonious. There is no thrilling, or heart stopping, or tragic way to reveal that something was 'lost on a walk' unless we are discussing children. It was an evening walk that rendered my glasses useless.

They had been removed from my face for a good chew. Sometime between there and my front door they'd fucked off to live with some toothless bitch perhaps named Doris.

JUSTICE FOR TEABAGS!

The other day I watched Black Swan (2010) and decided it was time for my villain era to begin. But the next day I refused a cup of tea. Thought the teabag might be able to feel itself burning to death. Thought perhaps I was not up to the job.

Then remembered the adrenaline rush I got from buying a cheese and onion sandwich from Tesco. As a villain, I would not care that cheese and onion has been shunned as a stinky person flavour. Be proud of your onion breath.

No one kisses villains anyway.

(Make It Into A Gay Person Bit About Disney's Obsession With Attributing Their Villains With Queer Characteristics!)

Don't be gay! Gay people will give you legs but tell you to shut up if you're straight and unappreciative of your FABULOUS mermaid tail!

(Make It Into A Gay Person Bit But Try To Overcome All Stereotypes!)

Your best friend told you, when you were eating your cheese and onion sandwich, that you were doing a good job of that.

Cheese and onion is, apparently, a very heterosexual choice in sandwich filling.

You should've been vegan.

They make great villains. Most of them are gay so everyone hates them already. It's not very fair. Most vegans will, admittedly, shut up about the moralities of the cheese and onion sandwich in favour of better breath than the person sat next to them. They would prefer for that role to be filled by someone else. It's not fair. But it's getting warmer.

For God's sake. Just have an iced tea.

THE PIGEONS COULDN'T HELP THEMSELVES

While the people at the party discussed cocaine, and the

weight of cocaine, and the smell of cocaine, and how

discussions of cocaine led to radness by osmosis,

we discussed ceiling fans. I asked if she had ever tried

looking up at a ceiling fan and spinning in the

opposite direction. She asked who the hell in England

owned a ceiling fan. I struggled. Between admitting to

the lie or having one in my possession. I told her I had

never tried it but could build on past experiences of

staring into the propellers of airplanes as I

cartwheeled home. My family had argued over the

value of Vaseline and whether or not they had it in

Spain.

HAD TO BRING MY DOG OVER. CUZ YOUR DOG HAS BECOME A SUPPORT DOG BY ASSOCIATION

NOW MY
DOG WON'T
STOP CRYING

AND TALKING
ABOUT THE
TIME HE CAUGHT
HIS OWN
TAIL!

LIKE IN THAT DOCTOR WHO EPISODE!

Some things in life make me feel really stupid :(

Like right now!

When I picked up my glass of water. Mother made me put it on a coaster. So, when I picked it up it got stuck on the coaster because someone said it was hot in England today. When I picked it up and it got stuck because of science I got this big rush of adrenaline. And, AND, after the coaster fell onto the floor and it clattered and made my dog wake up, I looked around and I thought: 'PHEW! Thank God no one was here to see that!'

Now my dog looks really depressed :(

There are other things in life that make me feel a bit less stupid. Like when you make an account on one of those websites where you do an exam to prove you are not a robot. I score 100% each time, and, AND, on a good day I'll get the one where you count busses.

When I was eleven, I took an exam that tested if I was clever enough to eat lunch at the same school as my sister. I cried on my first day and people kept on asking me what was wrong. A bit later I was taught that if I worked as hard at maths as I did counting busses then my sister might have shared her crisps that day!

:(

FEEL ABOUT U

THE WAY A RAISIN MUST

FEEL ABOUT A

CRANBERRY

x

AND NOW I WILL USE YOUR MIRROR TO PRACTICE FACIAL EXPRESSIONS

I pitched an idea to a hairdresser once. Asked if there were any way to fashion my hair from a towel so I would always have something to dry my hands with. She asked if I wanted a fringe- no she asked how often my hands were wet. I said 'often. I'm a spiller. Ask Mother, she enquired once about making me waterproof. I know. Lack of funding from the government. Plus. Waterproof babies, I've heard, are difficult. Takes purpose from the elbow and makes it sad. We did think, actually (and there was a lot of mind mapping involved), we thought maybe we could fashion something from clingfilm, but I started having nightmares about a man trying to put cheese and pickle in me. Oh.'

PART TWO: DISCUSSIONS OF THE POLY-POO

Together we came to the conclusion that none of it could be about Love Island (2019) due to issues in translation. Instead, my dog told me today that a week ago, as he had watched his polystyrene poo fly off into the sunset, that he had seen, stood atop the poly-poo, a tiny polystyrene man screaming for help.

I was pissed off. Couldn't stop screaming about how long it had been. He says, 'it's only been a week!' I say, 'yeah, but how long is that for you?' Worse, what would it translate to in time for the polystyrene man? I was pissed off.

But didn't know how to communicate any of it to a dog, so we just sat there in bed watching Love Island (2019).

A MISTAKE

SOMETHING
U MADE :̈

ASKING ABOUT THE XMAS ON MY HANDS

← THE MISTAKE

:)

PIXELS DON'T MAKE ME SNEEZE!

I am going to write a poem about abusive relationships. You don't have to have been in a relationship to relate to it. You can always think about that friend you never felt quite right about but you've been friends for ages so it would be awkward to stop now. And if you've never had a friend, you can think about all of the drugs and the alcohol that people say are harmful, but you actually think are quite lovely.

I've never liked cats. People gasp when I say things like that. But in my defence, I've been allergic my whole life. So, it kind of feels like they started it. Cartoon cats are okay though.

I heard a rumour about Tom and Jerry, actually. Don't tell anyone, but Tom's only chasing Jerry because he was bought to catch and kill him. They're actually very good friends, (or lovers, or glasses of wine). Tom knows that if he doesn't pretend to chase Jerry he'll be replaced by a meaner, nastier cat that will take his friend, or his lover, or his glass of wine to cartoon heaven. Then he'll be sad and depressed. It would be nice, for Tom at least, if while he was engaging in an elaborate scheme to keep Jerry alive-

It would be nice if Jerry would stop whacking him over the head with a baseball bat.

MY SLUTTY PAIR OF SLIPPER SOCKS

Mother does not like it when I fly around the house wearing nothing but slipper socks and a blanket cape. She tells me we are not an electric stove type of family. Had we been, I could run around clad in blanket cape to my heart's content making full use of my slipper socks. My slipper socks could never be happier. They would brag to all of the other socks of the holes in their souls from the friction of their slippering on the slippery kitchen floors and then the other socks, the jealous ones, would call them sluts, a pair of sluts, my slutty, slutty pair of slipper socks.

We are a gas stove type of family.

Mother grows concerned that one day I will set myself alight when slippering by. I tell her I am a person who learns from experience. It is like that time she told me not to sit on the top deck of the bus because she knew a woman who got mugged there and then I sat on the top deck of the bus and I became that woman.

I tell Mother that if she were a scientist everybody would shun her for not knowing when to celebrate. Mother argues that when a person is being engulfed by flames from a gas stove they have very little time to learn from their experiences. And that their mother has even less time to say, 'I told you so.'

Still. She somehow finds the time, among the audacity, to ask me (as I am leaving for work) to brighten everybody's day.

MY BROTHER'S GIRLFRIEND
CAME TO STAY

She and Tony the Tiger made friends immediately
because he's a social slut who wants to sell Frosties to
everybody. She poured the milk, not the cereal, into
her bowl first. I felt at risk. And then she opened the
microwave and put her bowl of Frosties inside of it to
die. Me and Tony shared a look. It was like we were
each other's camera in The Office (2003). Quite
romantic really. And then the microwave beeped, and
my brother's girlfriend sat down with her radioactive
bowl of Frosties and Tony smiled at her in the same
way that he smiles at me. Now I feel dirty and used.

HAVE STARTED STICKING
MY HANDS IN MEAT CHURNERS!
NOT IN A CRY FOR HELP KIND
OF WAY! WAS JUST HOPING
U MIGHT MISTAKE THEM
FOR SPAG BOL AND

RIGHTS FOR DUST MITES

Sometimes when I lie on the floor like this, I can feel the people in my carpet screaming for help. Something about how they're sick of being walked all over and the slaughter of their pet dust mites and something called the great hoover of 09.

(You Will Not Hear Them. You Have Been Looking Vertical In RECENT TIMES.)

I stopped listening for that last bit. They have resorted to poking little imprints and ridges into my cheek. I can feel your worry that they will be there forever. They won't. The prime minister of the carpet people told me. He offered a formal apology on behalf of his nation. But when he told me sorry, I couldn't help but notice the dents in his own face, so...

Sometimes when I lie on the floor like this, I think about all the things I could do to distract you from the ridges in my face.

(Like I Thought For This Next Bit I Could Start Coughing Up Bits Of Fluff As A Warning Of What Might Happen To The Carpet People Should They Repeat Past Mistakes.)

Thing Is I Have Made Being The Only Person In My Family Without Asthma A Bragging Point.

I say to the carpet people, sometimes, when I'm lying on the floor like this, I ask if they know we had the carpets done a few years back. I tell them there is probably another layer of carpet people beneath them who are equally, if not more, upset than they are because that's how carpet replacements work.
Now they're all screaming and trying to think of a way we can hide Homebase.

I ask if they'd feel better looking at samples or colour schemes to feel more included. They call me an idiot. I try opening up the hoover but all the dust mites are dead and there's no room for their bodies and apparently I have made the situation all the more upsetting. You call me downstairs for a meeting. Tell me to leave my bedroom empty. A man is coming over to look at the ceiling.

Last Week You Found A Woman In It.

FROZEN PEA UNDER YOUR FREEZER ABOUT TO HAVE AN IDENTITY CRISIS.

PART THREE: BACK ON THE POLY-POO

A pigeon attempts to mount it. This is the beginning of the end. It is not the weight of the pigeon that sends the poly-people to their tragic demise. But what the pigeon, with its politics and its blue-green colours represents: a whole ton of stuff of which the poly-poo-people could never comprehend. They jump. Hand in hand with a heavy sense of understanding that will finally align them with our laws of gravity.

☒ LOST MY EARPHONES
☒ DO SUNGLASSES BIT
☐ AGAIN?

YOU'LL KNOW THAT THIS ONE'S OVER WHEN I GAG

Got a six pack of yoghurt. Two peach. The others not-so-peach. I am yet to find a person to eat the four rejections. Even if I did the relationship would be dysfunctional. I don't want to share a fridge with someone who likes cherry.

Could get on board with a strawberry yoghurt consumer. As long as they did not consume in my vicinity or talk to me about it. Together we could watch the cherry yoghurts rotting like a sunset in a zombie apocalypse.

But the sunset would never go down! We would watch the cherry yogurts rot until they gave birth to flies that would eat them.

People cope with such things in different ways. I know a few who eat in times of crisis, but you already promised you would stop consuming strawberry yoghurt in my vicinity so you should probably start doing drugs.

Don't Know Why U Would Choose This Precise
Moment To Bring Up The Empty Jam Jar In The
Fridge? It Is A Token Of Our Guilt And A Reminder
To Do Better. I Say Sorry To It In Earshot Because I
Like Pity When I Can Pretend It Is Non-Consensual
You Are Full Of Ideas About Us Shutting The Fridge
But I've Never Been Good At Budgeting Besides Our
Differences Were Always Different For One Thing U
Like Strawberry YOgEURGHHHHHHHHHHHHHH
HHHHHHHHHHHHHHHHHHHHHHHHHHHHHHH
HHHHHHHHHHHHHHHHHHHHHHHHHHHHHHH
HHHHHHHHHHHHHHHHHHHHHHHHHHHHHHH
HHHHHHHHHHHHHHHHHHHHHHHHHHHHHHH
HHHHHHHHHHHHHHHHHHHHHHHHHHHHHHH
HHHHHHHHHHHHHHHHHHHHHHHHHHHHHHH
HHHHHHHHHHHHHHHHHHHHHHHHHHHHHHH
HHHHHHHHHHHHHHHHHHHHHHHHHHHHHHH
HHHHHHHHHHHHHHHHHHHHHHHHHHHHHHH
HHHHHHHHHHHHHHHHHHHHHHHHHHHHHHH
HHHHHHHHHHHHHHHHHHHHHHHHHHHHHHH
HHHHHHHHHHHHHHHHHHHHHHHHHHHHHHH
HHHHHHHHHHHHHHHHHHHHHHHHHHHHHHH
HHHHHHHHHHHHHHHHHHHHHHHHHHHHHHH
HHHHHHHHHHHHHHHHHHHHHHHHHHHHHHH

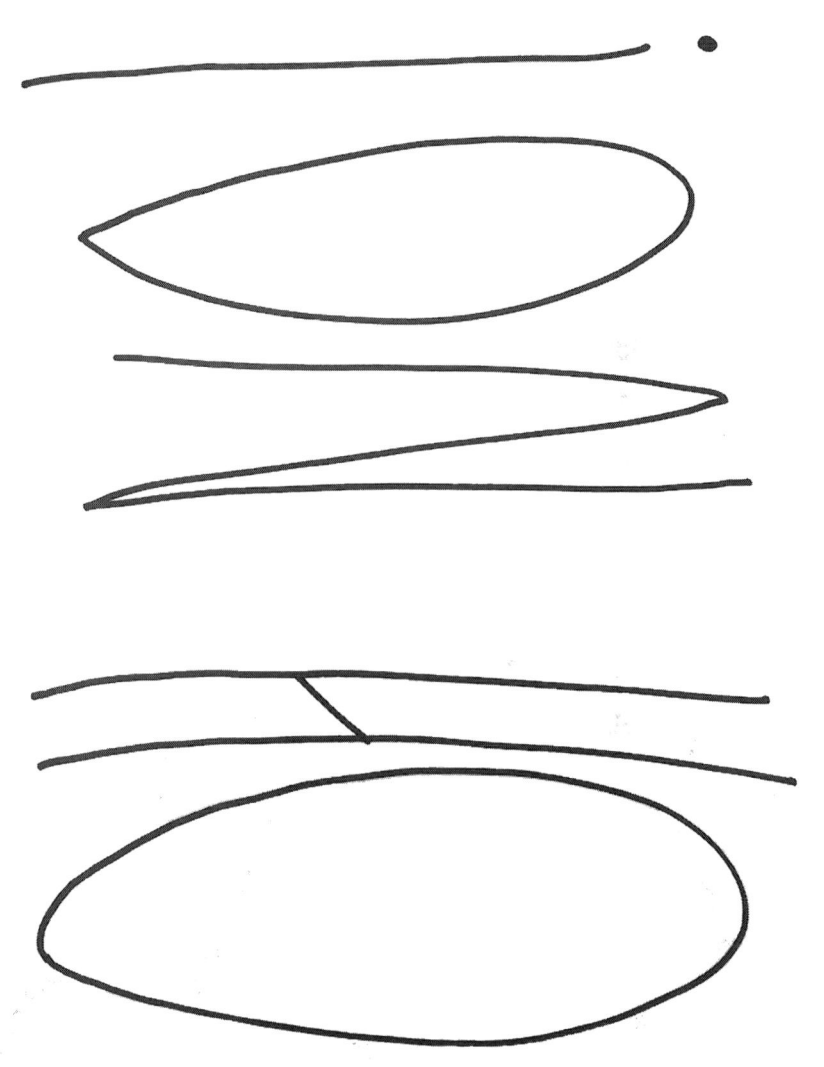

360 EQUALS A CIRCLE (BUT I DON'T THINK WE SHOULD BRING THE DEVIL INTO IT)

Somebody I kissed gave me a cold sore for free. Once I met this girl who got herpes from a guy that she slept with. When the girl with the herpes told me about the herpes we were stood in a sex shop.

I worked at the sex shop as a way to fund my travels between the sex shop and my house.

Soon it would become more than that. I progressed within the sex shop and as greed and ambition took over I would finally understand what it meant to be a true career bitch. People would introduce me to other people and say, 'it's worth the staring for the discount on lube.'

I told the girl with the herpes, after she told me about the herpes, that I could probably get her discounted condoms for life. Not that I was planning on staying at the sex shop for life. Though I might've done. For her.

At the time I thought we could do a bulk-buy kind of thing. That way her and my manager would like me more. The girl with the herpes told me it was too late for all that. But when I looked down at the pack of condoms in my hand they were still in date, so

I RECKON IF
WE LIVED IN
CAVEMAN TIMES
I WOULD HAVE TO
WALK ROUND IN A
NET OF ANTS
TO KEEP WARM

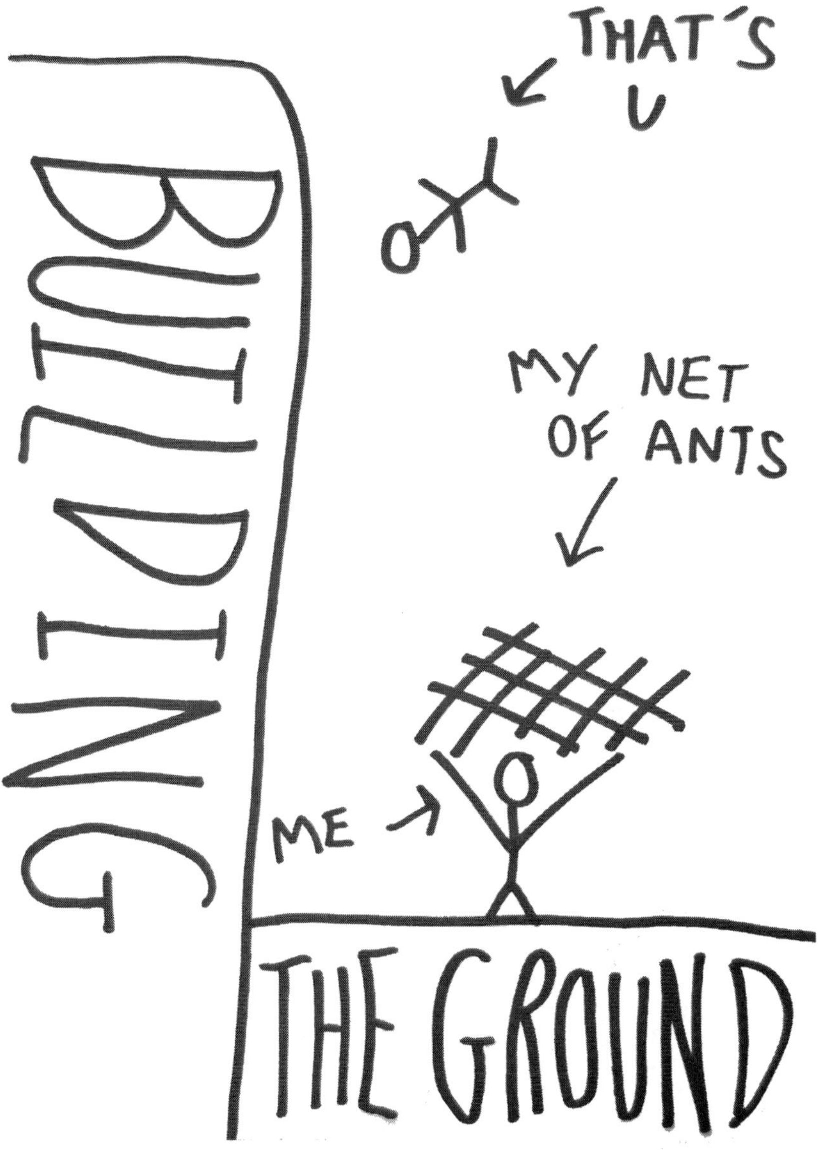
THAT´S
U
MY NET
OF ANTS
ME
BUILDING
THE GROUND

STILL GAGGING

Do you know what, at least the cherries have the decency to categorise themselves within my head as something I do not like. You are in pies, and jams, and I hate you. In sweets I'm not too fussed. Then you dip yourself in chocolate. I am erect. The other day you peeled the lid off a peach yoghurt and said it should be labelled as pre-consumed. It was a shame food. I would eat it at night with the lights off when everyone had gone to bed. Imagine waking up a yoghurt. I wouldn't like it either. Next time we will save ourselves the mess. Keep it in the freezer and feel good about ourselves when our married friends bring out the ice cream.

I'M NOT (I PROMISE)

At the end of a lead, I found a dog wearing a jacket that said 'nervous.' A close friend said that if I were the thing at the end of the lead then my jacket would read 'confused.' I said, 'I'm not kinky like that.'

A less-close friend disagreed. She told me my jacket would read 'lives in Birmingham.' I told the less-close friend that her jacket would read 'incorrect.' That I'd moved from Birmingham to Dublin a year ago because she wouldn't be able to tell that I was lying.

Both friends pissed off into a conversation about how everything would've been easier if God had a label maker. Sometimes I worry that he never meant to make us humans. We messed everything up with evolution.

He was happy cooking fish, until the fish took things into their own hands and then he was like 'God, where'd you get them?'

To be fair to God, whenever I visit the pet shop the names of the fish are always written on the walls of their tank. He probably wanted us to stay inside. I asked my friend what would be written on the wall of my tank. She said, 'we're not doing this again,' and I started, for the first time, to feel sorry for Jesus.

PROMISE (WHEN U (AND) NOT TO BRING UP THE ANTS?

U KNOW THAT
MIRROR IN UR ROOM?
LOOKS LIKE THIS

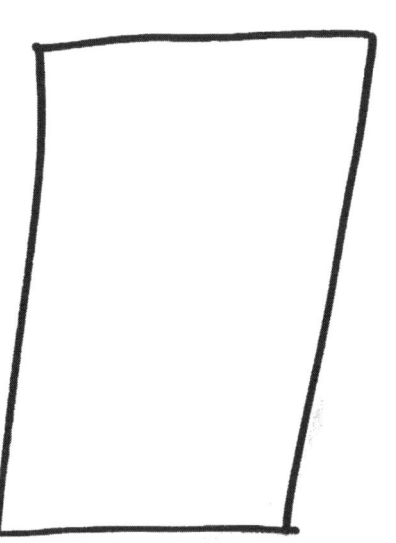

YEAH WAS
WONDERING
DID u MOVE IT
OR HAVE I
TURNED INTO A

PIECE OF WALL

THE SHOE ROOM

You took me into a separate room to show me new
shoes. I knew I would not like them. I was panicking.
Because I have a face that talks. The shoes upset me.
They couldn't decide, in the dark room, if they were
yellow or white. Neither would help my head. I'm a
messy eater. And I can't wear yellow, it clashes with
pasta sauce. I did not like your shoes. To stop my face
from talking I asked you if they were Nike. You said
of course not. And I couldn't stand that; you in your
shoes and me, wrong, at the end of it. I wanted to take
a big pen out and draw a tick on the shoes so at least
they would agree with me.

U TOOK ME TO A
DINNER PARTY I
WAS NOT INVITED
TO CUZ I COULDN'T
STAND THE WAY
THEY SWALLOWED

AND HOW IT
REMINDED
ME OF
THE

THINGS
IN THEIR
NECKS!

IT'S JUST DRY HEAVING NOW

Imagine being a yoghurt.

Big label on your head that says you are unsuitable for large groups of people.

THERE ARE
TIMES I WISH I
COULD GIVE U
SOMETHING MORE
PERSONAL, LIKE A
FAVOURITE NECKLACE
OR BLOOD TYPE

X

Am Feeding Them BISCUITS While They Sniff At The Fruit
Bowl.

Tell Them That Santa Once Punched A GAY ELF!

MY DOG

Rolls His Eyes And Stomps Off.

Ur Dog Looks At Me With Tears In Her Eyes

Tell Her She Is Not Supposed To Make Me Feel Think Of
These ThinGs.

She Sits Up Next To Me At The Table.

THE HOMOPHOBE

SHITS
EVERYWHERE

LOOKING RIGHT

You feel very sad crossing the road because there's a
Red Man and a Green Man and you think within that
there's probably a love story. You ask about it. Waiting
with the Red Man. You think, for a moment, that you
might be getting somewhere. But then the Green Man
arrives, and the Red Man's off. Because he lost, so.
You end up crossing the road with the Green Man
after that. Give him a dirty look on the Red Man's
behalf. Bastard just smiles. Red Man's chattier the
next day. Says it all blew up over some dinner. But
you reckon things had been tricky from the get-go.
Stuff about the Green Man always working late and
partying too hard and his obsession with being on the
go. The go's no good for anyone. Says the Red Man,
who'd only wanted to sit down and have a nice chat
about things. You tell him about the traffic lights. Ask
if he and the Green Man had ever considered adding a
third to balance things out. Trying not to sound too
eager. Just spontaneous, up for that sort of thing. You

know. But he takes one look at your cheeks and laughs. Things have changed between the two of you. Now you wait in silence. I believe that one day you will see the Green Man's side of things.

DOORS! DOORS! DOORS!

The villain is someone else entirely. Not me. My morals are fine. Thanks. It's doors. Doors are the enemy. Within them – in better words: either side – stands the opportunity for humiliation, or disappointment, or fear. Cinematic villains traditionally evoke at least one of these emotions within their protagonist. The humiliation of pushing a pull door for instance might represent the closeted school bully in a teen drama. We might recall, for argument's sake, the disappointment we all felt in Hugh Grant for what he did to Bridget Jones in Bridget Jones (2001). In door-form this might be like when your neighbour's Amazon package arrives on the other side of your door instead of your Amazon package or Hugh Grant or his package.

We needn't discuss doors and horror films.

But we will.

They are the culprit behind my mistrust of doors attached to fridges. I don't like the way the door and the light work together. Makes me feel ganged-up-on. And seems, to me, the perfect opportunity for all of the food inside to be murdered.

Things never work out for the food stood outside of the fridge either. There always seems to be someone hiding behind the fridge door, so when the protagonist has finished thinking about snacking, and closes it, everybody watching goes:

AH!

Thanks.

That's not it. But I appreciate you staying this long.

Thanks.

Wish I could stop thanking you.

But I am learning it is better to be thankful than sorry when someone exits through a door. Because you always learn something, (even if it is just what the back of that person's head looks like).

Going to talk about doors some more.

Don't want to but feel like we were getting somewhere.

And the only way to get anywhere, really, is usually through a door so.

STILL DOORS!

They will never be unvillanous. They may have gotten me to this point, which happens to be slightly better than the last. But if a murderer bought me a birthday cake I would not feel comfortable blowing out my candles and leaving myself in the dark with him.

Should stop expecting the doors to change. Wonder if when I change, myself, the doors will begin to fear me. Wondered that once, actually. Then dismissed the thought as ridiculous and absurd.

They do not think of me. There will be no attempt, once I have passed through, to continue the war. No efforts to trick. I will not wake up one day to find all the 'push' and 'pull' signs have been swapped to read 'kick' and 'headbutt.'

Hugh grant will never hide behind my fridge door. And if he does, I will know who murdered all the food. And even though I would be disappointed in Hugh I would not be scared. He has enough money to restock it.

And I would tell Hugh to tell the doors that I was never scared. And that even if I had been scared, I am not scared anymore, and even if I had been scared anymore I would be brave enough not to show it and at some point brave enough to show it but-

THE DOORS ARE NOT CONTEMPLATING ANY OF THIS BY THE WAY!

Neither is Hugh. The doors do not think of me. Or Hugh. They are doors. Perhaps within that (EITHER SIDE) there is a quality to be admired.

END

DO THE ☐ ☐ CARS KNOW ☐ THEY ARE ☐ SOCIALISING ☐ OR ARE WE ☐ IN A CAR PARK

ACKNOWLEDGEMENTS

MUM DAD ELLIE LOUIS ZIGGY RIP BRADLEY BETH FI
SOF JEM ISH MR RAY JENNY ZAKI MAGGIE NATHAN
GRACIE CALLUM ANDREW SCOTT COUSCOUS CAPITAL
LETTERS SHARPIE PENS NOT MY BEDROOM MORETTI
MY HAIR AND ALL OF MY HATS. [OH AND STU I 'SPOSE]

LOVE YOU X

WRITE YOUR OWN CHEESE AND ONION SANDWICH POEMS HERE:

ABOUT VERVE POETRY PRESS

Verve Poetry Press is a prize-winning press that focused initially on meeting a local need in Birmingham - a need for the vibrant poetry scene here in Brum to find a way to present itself to the poetry world via publication. Co-founded by Stuart Bartholomew and Amerah Saleh, it now publishes poets from all corners of the UK - poets that speak to the city's varied and energetic qualities and will contribute to its many poetic stories.

Added to this is a colourful pamphlet series, many featuring poets who have performed at our sister festival - and a poetry show series which captures the magic of longer poetry performance pieces by festival alumni such as Polarbear, Suhaiymah Manzoor-Khan and Imogen Stirling.

The press has been voted Most Innovative Publisher at the Saboteur Awards, and has won the Publisher's Award for Poetry Pamphlets at the Michael Marks Awards.

Like the festival, we strive to think about poetry in inclusive ways and embrace the multiplicity of approaches towards this glorious art.

www.vervepoetrypress.com
@VervePoetryPres
mail@vervepoetrypress.com